The Bird Hospital

Anna Wigley

First Impression—2002

ISBN 1 84323 068 2

© Anna Wigley

Anna Wigley has asserted her right under the Copyright, Design and Patents Act, 1988, to be identified as Author of this Work.

This book is published with the support
of the Arts Council of Wales.

Printed in Wales at
Gomer Press, Llandysul, Ceredigion SA44 4QL

CONTENTS

ACKNOWLEDGEMENTS

Some of these poems first appeared in the following magazines and anthologies: *New Welsh Review, Poetry Wales, Poetry Review, Fire, Iota, Links, Borderlines, Advance, The New Writer, Oxygen, Exeter Anthology 1999, Ragged Raven Anthology 1999, Poetry Nottingham.*

Duck-shooting

That was the summer you took me
on gunmetal mornings, early,
to strange deserted places:

wet ground, forests of rushes,
hard grass stubbling
from a sodden mattress.

Mindful of my privilege
I was silent as instructed,
trod softly in the wake

of your long legs and galoshes.
In the holster of your hip
the butt of your rifle jogged.

Toads the colour of mud
panted silently on mud ledges.
We caught the electric trace

of a snake. No wind.
Just a cold smell of water
and the sky getting lower.

On a jigsaw of cracked sludge
you crooked a knee,
patted me down, slid the catch;

I saw nothing but the back of your head
as you leaned like a cat
into the eye of the sight,

clenching yourself round the gun
until you had it tamed,
and with a slow squeeze let death out.

The ducks were soft and loose
as bundles of silk.
Their rainbowed necks

lolled from the mouth of your bag.
Later we would pick the shot
from the stopped hearts

be soldierly and not mind
the sick tug of quills from flesh,
the high pyre of feathers.

Moss

I had never seen the colour green
until the Long Mynd moss
lay at my feet in a cold rain,
burning;

as if some temperamental goddess
had turned out her jewel-box
here, on this stubbled heath

then set fire to the lot.
And this was what was left:

the just-cooling embers and coals
still on their necklace-strings,
curling like miniature constellations
in a fern-and-heather heaven.

Wenallt

The path through the beech wood
goes downwards
through tide-falls of clay
between sparse birch saplings
and flotsam of ivy netting
and drab tenacious flowers –
white drone blossoms
trailing from ground mud;

crooks and falters and loses itself
in basketing shadows
and a floor that stumbles
from tier to half-tier

but is definitely there
though blurred – a baldness
of some length and consistency

strung with the tread of hooves:
soft watery hollows
by the fallen birch trunk
with its strangely twisted flesh;

and it keeps going downwards
at a cautious slant
across the forested steepness to the right,
the beeches striking up
from the plunging bank
like stiff serried masts of ships
in a disused, forgotten port.

Dusk Horses

The loss of light lent them power,
brought their bulky haunches
and the cranes of their heads closer.

They belonged to the smoky hour
more than we did;
the dark air stroked their flesh
with softened hands
and the grass was sweeter, cooler.

One raised his head slowly
like the prow of a ship
yawing up through the waves
of the blackening field,

and turned back his eyes as if
a ghost had mounted him
and he staggered for balance.

Showing us for a moment
a Parthenon profile, marble-massy
and near, he stalled us –

we gripped the fenceposts,
seeing the field, the covening trees,
the darkness, were a place
where his name was changed

and we were foreigners
wandered from our map,
with neither castle nor inn
in sight, to lodge us.

Gorse

Through the cold months
the gorse is hot,

floating its flame
on frost-bitten cliffs,

burning all night
its yellow coals

on pine-green piles
of thorny sticks;

glowing to itself
on sides of hills

where passing sheep
with yellow eyes

beard the barbs
with wires of wool.

Swifts at Nightfall

The thickening shadows excite them;
and the cloud-shreds pulled to thin
streaks of purple washed with rose.
Hedgerows, sky, and fields

are their theatre, dimly lit,
a hall for their nocturnal aerobatics.
Swooping as sharp as knives
hurled fast, through the half-light,

they soar and dive, or skim a path
swift as a fearful glance
or kiss, across the river's width.
For a moment, looking up,

you might catch their fork and blade
stencilled black against the black;
or feel a confusion of quickness
tangling above you like wind.

The Bird Hospital

It found you always
when you tramped the woods and barns –
the broken bird;

like Fagin stashing loot
in the chambers of his pockets
you closed your big coat

round a tremble of feathers
and all the way home cooed
and lullabyed to it.

Then in the dim nursery
of your room, you let it free
to drag claw or wing

a few feet; to see again
its quick heaves at the weight
pulling it down.

For weeks you were mother and nurse,
your patience and cunning
coaxing from a bundle of fright

a bold nipping, the tatters
of an appetite. A column of water
from a dropper,

a sponge of bread, finally
a crumb of raw meat
swabbed its throat.

You stroked its bright back
with one crooked finger,
enquiring anxiously

into the tension of a splint;
woke in the night
to scrabblings from a box,

threw a shawl of whisky
over unimaginable fears.
Often it died

your brave intern,
the fight leaking from it
like a dripping faucet.

One morning the eyes would be milked,
the spring of the legs cut.
You buried it tenderly

without tears, your red fingers
angrily clawing a plot
under the spread wing of a tree.

Even at Noon the Copper Beeches

Even at noon the copper beeches
are secretive and dark, hiding
in their grape-black leaves
depth upon depth of shadow.
They are not quite natural;
like jungle plants strangely painted.
But with silky thin ruffles
that hardly make a sound in the breeze.
And at dusk: then the copper beeches
inhabit their own purple light,
and stand like gentle titans
in the unpeopled park, growing bigger
under the strange touch of the night.

Spider

Hammocked
between four frail twigs
he practises stillness;

brooched
on his metropolis of threads
he straddles the wind;

like shingle under a wave
lets the air take him
almost.

Waits
as if waiting itself
were the purpose.
Rests lightly as a raindrop
on the hub of his life
in his eight perfect senses.

A blundering hand
sends him hobbling to the edges
of naked air,
his castle ruined;

tomorrow he will crochet another
as carefully as before

paddling himself
in decreasing circles
towards a new, still centre.

Blackbird

Sleek priest-suited rustler
of bushes and back-lawns,
always holding some information, urgent,
in his listening circles of eyes
and carrying it, quick,
to some place where he can bury it.

Sharp detective of the herb-gutters
and cat-concealing shrubs,
scuttering from muggings,
sounding the all-red siren of his
stone-chipping flint from a wall-top.

Then in the porcelain hour
before dusk, pulling posy after posy
of trefoil and scarlet pimpernel
from the field in his breast.

Blue Hydrangea

after Rilke

Rust has spotted them: now they stand
like the innards of a clock,
their frail propellor blooms
exposed to corroding rain.

Yet each flat petal stays intact
on its stalk, the whole head
keeps its first exuberant dome.

They are not entirely drained
of their azurian inks blurring
through a dozen nameless shades
to sugar pinks and spearmint:

a blotch of blue still battles there
on the edge, with a creeping brittleness:
as if unwilling to surrender
this last defiant outpost.

The Goldcrest

We found him in the gutter, shrammed,
his thin stiffened feet turned up
like a dying man's hands above the sheet.

In the palm he was light as a leaf,
a bare ounce of barely-beating life.
We laid him in a coffin-cradle box
to thaw out his tickering pulse.

By morning an August of heat
had done it. His wings whirred
and a motor spun free in his breast.
He lifted like a moth and fluttered
from his tomb of cardboard,

landed on a skirting twig
and rested there, quite still,
rediscovering his breath.
The lick of yellow paint on his head
had a warrior look;
his spider-feet gripped the world.
And his tiny beak was a comb again
to make himself smart with.

Heavenwards

What cliff-edge were we marooned on
by the wind in the night? We woke
from shallow sleep to find the house
perched on a fraying ledge

and every minute loosening itself
by a few more crumbs, leaning
outwards into the wind's arms
as if hypnotised and tired

of its sedentary life.
We bore down in our beds,
gravity-loving and wishing
we were hill-heavy and welded

to an earth whose nuts and bolts
were rattling loose. But some
centrifugal malevolence
had plans for us and was focussed

with white-hot intent
on blasting us into space.
The house was an origami hut
hanging on by a paperclip;

it was a candle flame snatched
and funnelled to impossible thinness,
dragged from the tiny tether
of its wick. It was like that

all through the hours of blackness
as we crouched unsleeping,
tensed round a scrap of groundforce,
waiting to be torn loose and flung

into a whirligig of roofs and trees,
where we could no longer do anything
but be stirred, with sudden loss of weight
towards heaven, like the first stars.

Moth

Creature of dust and powder;
weightless as a wisp of fluff

blown now against my window
in the navy blue hour

to suck on light, like a bee
drunk in a sunflower.

For a moment you rest,
your wings like scraps of silk,

and show me all the bulk
and tangle of your underside:

the old velvet corset,
the confusion of wires.

The glass holds you up
like a section on a slide,

and sensing such hardness
lies across your heart's path

you palpitate off,
fretting and fussing

through the penetrable dusk.
But soon you're back

pulled on a string
to your 60 watt love.

Infatuated, blinded
by brilliance, you would die

for your glass pearful
of electric white;

so you petition the pane,
hopeful as only lovers are,

craving the brief flaring
of a gross passion

over the safety
of the long, familiar night.

In the Castle Grounds

Gaudy as transvestites
the peacocks float

their long torpedoes
of petrol blue,

opera singers' eyes
painted for twilight

sightings
from turreted rooms.

Haughty and rapt
as Sitwells in smoking suits,

bold from the pages
of Beardsley and Wilde,

they pace the lawns
like dowagers,

last exhibits of an age
of disdainful indolence,

when their high-strung cries
were thrown like banners

over the ramparts,
and the coffers of their tails

opened idly to amaze
with a sunburst of coins.

The Leopard

He opens like a bullet from a gun:
appearing in terrible, immediate speed
from a statue of crouched stone.

Violence from stillness: as a thunder clap
seizes the sky by the neck-scruff
and furiously shakes it;

but also as an enamelled butterfly,
from the dead, dusty, folded
bookends of its moment's rest
whirrs suddenly in a papery blur
of Titian golds and reds.

★　　★　　★

The mind at perfect rest –
in fact hardly present,
but settled like a fisherman's fly
on the surface of a deep lake.

His body neatly tucked
to the shape of his contentment:
balanced, symmetrical, precise.

His concentration
without strain, on some invisible rope
running beneath the pads of his feet,

and some inaudible music
playing a concerto in his brain –
one in which each phrase echoes
and rebounds in spheres
through the hillocks of his shoulders
and his haunches' rolling fields.

Seals

Iron-grey under the webbing,
the water sends up a sting of salt
and the white air is whiter.

The seals, half-fish, half-cat,
perch weirdly on the rocks
and complain of broken promises.

Their long, Edwardian necks
raise them above the shoulder-stumps
that swipe at the land, and sway them
like the prows of small, lost ships.

Why were they brought here,
to be thrown half-formed and mewing
on the sharp-knuckled rocks?
Their eyes bulge black marble
dredged from the deep;
their whiskers are long as reeds.

No wonder they cry to return
to the sea's springy net,
where a hundred hands rise up
to catch them as they are launched
and carried off: in that moment
when their noses break through water

they become swift dancers,
and the swagging of their tails lifts
lightly as Pavlova's foot.

Prelude

Before dawn a bar of birdsong
glances through the dark
experimentally, like a fish
rippling in and out of a cave;
or someone calling up the stairs
in a derelict house.

Magnolia

It's what
the black branches
endure for,

eleven months,
erupting
into this flock

of flamingoes balanced
in blue air,
their long feathers

moulting to pale nests
only days
from their opening

under harebell skies.
It is this flight
without movement

through April ether,
this cool bonfire
burning in silence

of fresh leaf
and incense;
singeing to a litter

of rusted
rubber tongues;
then the rough clasp

of another winter
before the birds
with their rose tints

roost again here.
How short their stay is
and how spendthrift.

Summer Morning

The invisible wood pigeon
sounds an exhausted note
from his broken wood-pipe.

The cypresses hoard the last dark,
still wrapped in their coolness.

Dew-beads abacus
a decagon of spider-mesh
in the holly hedge.
Daisy heads

dream late on the curtained lawn,
still clammed in sleep.

Night silence creeps
from the stones, gives way
to a faint warm stain.

A cat goes daintily
without noise
between fence-hurdles.

Bluebells

A fragment of May sky
has fallen here, and dangles now
in these Tiffany flowers.

A deep-stained shard
of cathedral window
has got buried in this patch
of wasteland shade,
and the stems spring from it.

No lamps could glow
in the woods' noon twilight
or the cool stone shadows
of the graveyard
as these flowers glow –
dark, phosphorescent –

like electric fish
lighting a dimly brilliant path
through dusky fathoms.

★   ★   ★

Nourished on grit and gloom
on corners and patches untended
even by the sun

sprouting between corpses
in the unmown aisles of graveyards

seeking unvisited shade
cadging a ride
on a crumbling wall, or stowing away
in hedges
where their tousled heads flounce
outrageously blue

they are finally at home
in a crowd of their own kind
under a copse on the hill

where, for a month,
passers-by catch their breath
at the violet field.

The Songbirds

Exiles from a vanished world
of intricate brightness; escapees
from the last Book of Hours,
where they woke to skies of unpolluted blue
and dived through them like angel fish,

these silk-embroidered birds
unspool from tiny throats
their gold and vermilion threads.
More swiftly than the petrol sheen
from their feathers widens the eye,
the song goes up,

an instantaneous tapestry minutely worked
with colours cool as mercury,
and hot as molten brass.

So delicate, a hand's embrace
could snuff the guttering candle of the heart
in its eggshell case,

so finished in each detail, a crest
might serve for Thumbelina's fan,

they quiver for a second
on the edges of our world
like momentary effects of light.

The Prothonotary Warbler

Like a teardrop of molten gold
hottest at the head, then cooling
to a tail of glossy slate

he fixes black-ribboned feet on bark
and tugs at grubs from hollows
in the trees over swamps and lakes.

Named for the Catholic scribes
with yellow robes, he writes
his own characters on the air
in perfect letter-strings:

his weet-weet-weet a manuscript
of bright, unbroken notes;
himself an exquisite drawing
radiant in the margins.

Barafundle

A mile from it the roads
narrow to a makeshift roughness.
The hedgerows have a thorny
suffering look, and birds are sparse.

We jolt and bounce
over the cratered, single track
with its middle of white dust.

Then one last twist brings us
at once into a new universe:

a wrenching-up of cliffs
from a gorge of shadow
and a sea
like a crystal continent.

Gulls glide in slow dreams
over the vast rock.
Here we might leave earth, touch sky;
we have stumbled
on one of the world's edges,
with amazed breath.

October

Carves the thorn
chisels the leaf
frets the iron
of the oak and beech;

glazes the rosehip
hardens the haw-pip
waxes the holly
toughens the husk;

then rolls it all
in an ash of frost
and whets it quick
on a stone of light.

Cyclamen

They kept themselves for last –
tiny cones rolled tight
as the end-twists of cigars.

Not until a cold mist
touched them awake, did they light
their frosted lamps;

then theirs was the only colour
in the chrome steel months;
never drooping, never rusting,

but each morning fresh, and there,
delicately bright;

petals of mist
a fragile-seeming promise
in November catacombs,

of the coming, flickering light.

November 1st

The park's turned planetarium:
a thousand yellow stars hang
startling in the shadows.
Comets of ash and alder
blaze golden trails; limes
suspend heart-shaped satellites.
Beeches expire over light years
in rosy explosions;
the tulip tree's a sun whose flame
reaches beyond all others.

Boxing Day to Lydney

After the night's slow
tempera of crystal and flake

laying layers of silence
white on white,

the valley is painted
at shoulder and hip:

a voluptuously sequinned
starlet in Versace.

The quiet has gathered
on paw-pads of firs,

sprayed stones with salt,
left grass blades sugared,

laid a line of white
on the meanest twig.

By dawn the birches
are sculptures of ice,

silver-scarved necks
rustling heads of lace.

The fields are white lakes
of coconut milk

below an acre of blue
with the lid blown off.

Under the trees, noon
lays small black knives.

After Snow

Step out
into the white heart of silence.
This night has brought it
whole, into the open
and all at once:

an imperial stillness,
and the tireless insignia
of snow on smallest objects:
wispy weeds, railing-spikes.

Nothing is spared, no leaf
is without its cornicing,
no brick without its crust.

The crooked shapes of twigs
have their highlights;
the holly's scallop
is faithfully preserved.

Distant blue-white slopes
lie calm as windless fjords.

Penarth, January

Behind us the pale sea
of melting sun; cold deliquescence
of a tarnished salver.

But in its shadow –
a canvas of such tender colour
as might have been harvested
from dragonfly and kingfisher.

We drive into it
as into a receding mirage;

climbing the hill
are pierced with soft spears
of paper-cut trees,
their fretwork fragile
as black snowflakes

against a sky
deeper in all its dimensions

– as if it had just unsheathed
wings still wet with newness
and of such light, sifted stuff,
a dreaming gull might float

through all its tints
and never meet a boundary
of cloud or current

or blue or pink.

Crocuses

Cold flames
blossoming from cold grass
in the nettled wind.

A shiver of chilly sun
has brought them to the surface;
all year they have waited,
their gold and purple fires
banked; thin silks of flame
trampled to tatters by the rain

to rise again perfect
as new porcelain,
their little chalices
clean as March sunlight,
bright as courage.

The Aran

This woman's hands recall her grandmother's:
a pair of billing doves, crouched close
in her lap, weaving wool in their beaks.

The threads are thick as twine, and oiled
good as a seagull's weatherproof.
On rainy coastal walks they will hold out.

Under her darting fingers the twisting ribs
cable down like currents in rivers,
the broad ropes of fast-running water.

Heavy as a corpse it will be, this sweater.
Already it slumps at her feet like a dead man
whose lungs are sodden sponges.

She patterns for her own pleasure:
tapestries from this coarse, dun stuff
a rune of insinuating roads and ribbons.

Each garment is still its own signature.
But now no-one will know the owner
by his woollen markings. Her grandmother

knitted shrouds for unlucky sailors,
each man's name wrung from the briny stitches
when a storm took his face and changed it.

Miner

The lamps swing me through the narrow streets,
their ragged glinting lines like lanterns
bobbing on a dark lake.

Already my face feels black,
as night opens its mouth
and I prepare to sink

into deeper darkness,
down a throat of pitch.
For twenty years the black fat

of this valley has been my lot;
I have dug it out by inches
with the spade of myself

till my limbs were like timber,
knotted and hard.
Each day I drop

plumb, like a diver with a tank,
only once coming up for breath.
My skin's deflowered in minutes

and each hour deepens
my livery of soot
as I walk the tunnels of glossy rock,

close to the echo of my own breath,
the beak of my pick making blunt music,
my eyes like speedwells in the dark.

In the Romanian Bath-house

An underworld gloom; a limbo light
spilled through the loose seams of dreams
in this windowless acre
where naked feet slap echoes to the roof.

Avalonian veils gather and dissolve
their ghosts, dressing and undressing
the shoulders and breasts of the women
in cyclical striptease.

To these caves of forgiving mist
each week they come, Venuses
remaindered, whose ancient status
is restored with their quivering descent.

They are in their bodies at last,
in their pale belly mounds
and white-tented thighs.
They stir in the water slowly

like fabulous trout dreaming
through the mirrors of still pools.
And the water pays gentle court
to their every part, making satin islands

of knees, sea-fronds of hair;
slipping bracelets over their wrists.
When they return to the world above,
camouflaged in uniform shrouds,

do they remember their watery selves:
relive the slip into the water's glove,
lock themselves behind bathroom doors,
hide their redundant flesh like gills?

The Cellist's Fingers

At six her body arranged itself
around the voluptuous wood.
She learned the light embrace
of knees, the rapturous neck.
By nine her arms circled the notes
with tensile strength. The bow
carved in slow thrusts
and the phrases fell even and exact.
It was her shape-shifting hands –
the right a loose, light touch
on the ship's wheel, the left a spider
with tormented legs –
that felt the difference most.
On days when she did not play
she thrummed the stem of her arm,
the strings of her fingers pulled
by the strings in her head.
In civilian clothes her hands
looked normal: twiddled hair,
pulled plugs, fell into old
prolonged caresses.
Though now there was something new
in the way she held her spoon:
from above, at an angle to the wrist.
At twenty there were soles
like slippers on her fingertips;
but the nerves' telegraph
still carried the news fast
of the cavernous, touchy response.
This was her hands' work now:
a passionate domination,
commanding in stringent flurries
the great battalions.

The Jazz Pianist

Before he sits at the keys he seems
short-breathed with bulk:
his belly a whale, his arms fat fish
that struggle to hang straight.

He takes the slender stool between his legs
and perches: a buffalo on a shooting-stick.
The hands come up and rest
over the keys in dainty readiness.

Then he pulls from the piano's throat
with such a deft, exquisite touch
brilliant scarves; and we stare
as if the room were full of strange weather.

The Ex-Driver for the NKVD

There were two teeth left in his head
that showed like tent pegs when he smiled
which he often did.
He smiled when he told how he got the job
or was got for it; and the van was big,
a windowless bus.
Putting a loose-skinned hand
to his sunken chest, he recalled
daily ferryings to nameless fields;
fields where the blunt grass parted
for crudely-hacked trenches.
He was just a driver: that was where
his job description stopped.
And he was always conscientious.
I was always conscientious
he said, holding onto the words
like the last planks of a raft.
Then his teeth poked again from his gums
as he described the warm boots
standard issue, and hat.
Scuttling off, he returned with it,
holding it like some object
magically unaged, from beyond.
Placing it on his bald head
with the ghost of a flourish
he secured for us his place in history,
with a proud but puzzled look:
was that me? was it really that easy?

Trace

Because it led to nothing but
my watching you depart
one morning, straight as a dancer
as you mounted your bike
not looking back

am I then to forget
those silent nights spent
in your small, bachelor house –
its walls simple and fresh
as your best self;

its almost-single bed
a neat confession
of your bare-boarded life
and lightly furnished heart.

At the Handel Concert

There was a moment

after the small, plain church
had been filled to the ends of the pews
like a ship on a long voyage
to the New World

after the faces had placidly settled
to the soprano's brave tremor
like a vigorous, callow breeze
over the smooth, harmonious weather
of the first chorales

after the halfway mark was reached
with distant, polite half-smiles
and discreet rearrangements of behinds
on the polished oak seats

there was a moment

when all the singers struck up
together,
and woke the church to ecstasy;
like cloud cover clearing suddenly
from a splendour of echoing hills.

Frank

That day we visited
and you were in your chair
at noon, in your dressing gown;

your feet already past shame
in the intimate slippers,

the cavity of your chest
beneath the wool, unfleshed
like the bare stone of a fruit;

we shot arrows of gossip
and brandished our teacups
at the wild silence.

You indulged us,
being at one with the silence –
you alone had made friends with it.

It was why you shrank
into that strange frail smile,
your new, bird-small face
rosy and remote.

When we left
you were still wearing it
and turned it to me like a promise:

it's not so very bad,
my new address;
let's not pretend I won't be there
when you next visit.

Funeral

A fresh wound opened in the ground:
a raw, shaved, muddy patch
like a hole for rubbish, and as yet
no monument to mark the place.

After the golden church
this impoverished homecoming:
a dark slot dug by unknown hands,
a bare room lost among numerous rooms,
a cold hive of silent strangers.

The Finnish Woman

She has come among us like a silence
as if she feared to disturb us.
Her face is round as a child's,
and though she hardly speaks

her cheeks are an exclamation
of permanent flame. Hair bright
as flax falls from her brow
where a blonde heart is licked.

Is it shyness that she carries
like her blondness – that makes
her every footfall a dance step
to outwit noise, her voice

when it comes poised and quiet
as water balancing at the brim
of a glass, her pink hands
like slow, careful animals

that shrink from bright light?
Or is it some Finnish way
of preserving oneself like a pool
of stillness in a hurtling world –

the mind like a great lake
glass-smooth and cool;
the body both sacred and useful,
carrying silence like a jewel?

Feet

I was alarmed to see your feet
poking so sharp and naked
from your trousers, in the moonlight.
They were like pale, clawed animals
and they were unfamiliar –
I almost felt there were three of us.
How could you think it meant nothing
to spring that nakedness on me
unasked, unprepared for,
when to my dazzled senses
even your ears were sacred?

Meetings on June Evenings

There were the usual things,
like the staples of an old myth:
three letters, a summer moon,
and cacophonous silences.

Such silences!
For months we carried them round,
took them out when we were alone,
showing them like the last

two pearls in the whole world.
Those minutes were the busiest
we'd ever spent, so busy
we had to stay absolutely still

while they roared through us.
We were marooned together
on a ledge of earth
leaning out into the sky:

an immensity of black
pressing hard on a few stars.
When I dared to look
into your plundering eyes

I was stripped and rifled
of my last words.
Inside us, unfolding
their fathoms, the black spaces.

Napoleon's Horse

She stood no taller than he did
in his folded-pancake hat:
the outline of a horse with lifted head,
stalled at last after months
with the Emperor's small heels
nuzzling her gut, the snaffle
nagging at her soft mouth.

Her bones were there to touch –
crumbs shaken loose by chance
from a fold in history's skirts.
Having lived a legend
they had fetched up here intact;
like a tuft of Jason's fleece
tagged and mounted on a plinth.

We circled her slowly,
holding her voodoo charm
at arm's length; for suddenly
we were brought so close,
we thought we could discern
in the rattlesnake of her neck
the imprint of his soothing strokes

as he slowed her to a halt
at the last high place before the drop
to the field; and stooping,
breathed encouragement in her ear,
passed his palm over the silks
of mane and nape, then pincering
her chest, gathered the reins tight.

Levin looks for Kitty on the Ice

The crowd is thick with her absence.
I have come here
tugged by a string of fate
deliberately to place myself
in the sweep of her looks,

to be accidentally lighted-on.
I think I see her in every slim shape
gliding from the tangle of cloaks
that swoop about me gently
like circling rooks.

Those that are not her, I hate:
how can they be at peace
whether she comes or not?

A boy, slim as a ferret,
is carving parabolas on the ice.
His feet lead him with enchanted ease
and he follows, amazed,
gathering to a leap that twirls him
like a windspun seed.

She has not come. Flushed faces
sweep past me at a rush.
Coat-tails flick at my legs.

The sun is all milked over,
the air is spored with dark.
My legs go like an old man's,
paltry, devoid of sense.

She gave me a bright look once.
Could I have mistaken
such a glance?

A figure like the others
but so unlike the others
separates off, towards me.

And here she is.
Bodies brush by,
beautiful, benevolent. Snowflakes
have speckled the collar of her coat.

Sleep

Sleep takes her as a swan
slow-gliding in perfect balance
gathers in her cygnets like flakes
of herself that have wandered;

it extends a silent wing
so soft, its first brush
against her is hardly felt;
she is being folded in

to its thickly quilted breast
where all proud loneliness,
all energy and fret
against the low and dark

are swallowed up in deep
voluptuous blindness.
The heraldic wings close;
the lake is a dense black magnet.

Beloved Daughter

The crows that perch on her stone
are older than she was.
Their caws go over
her scant twenty inches.

What would she have made
of this maze of graves?
She would have recognised silence,
rain, gently amniotic,
and tiny muffled thuds.

And the air would have stirred
some memory of being wheeled,
just once, outdoors.

But greenness and birds,
and trees like living houses,
and the sky (not even handled
with a word)

— these she now lies under
like her last home,
though she did not stay
long enough to meet them,
and knew neither feather nor stone.

The Dark Escort

to Iris Murdoch

That's what your husband called it –
as if you were going to a ball
on the arm of a long shadow.

From these pictures you are absent.
Just as someone who is drunk
disappears from his face

so, here, you have been eaten
by a woman who stole your nose
and rifled your wardrobe

but fails to convince.
Comparing them with another –
half a life before –

where you seem to rebuke the camera,
caught like a fierce creature
between kills, your eyes

again absent, but this time
trained within, to feast
on some hidden, elaborate banquet,

it's as if a fire that burned
too furiously, was put out
by some envious act;

as if your eyes,
because they saw further than most,
had been quenched by a peevish god.

Archaeology

Clearing out,
I find maps of the past:

perfume phials
stoppering purple nights,

lurid tales from the mouths
of lipstick stubs.

Papyrus pages
brittle and smoked:

the thoughts of someone
I knew once.

In a sealed chamber,
letters from an unripe heart

and an unexploded photo
trailing loose wires.

Stillborn handkerchiefs
stiff-folded in a pack,

a fossil of glass
that once lived round my neck.

Two pressed pansies
disinterred from a book;

a spotted sixpence
weighing extremely light.

After the Op

Now as never before
he inhabits his body.

Adrift, he navigates
by pain's strict compass,

a calendar of drips and jabs,
the charts that trace

in jagged routes
his homeward journey.

Poised at the invisible fence,
we concentrate on the scenery –

the pressed blue sheet
failing to cover his foot;

the table he cannot reach,
the water he must not touch.

He regards us from a distance,
kindly. He was never so wise.

An incision in his spirit
has aged him into patience overnight.

And all I can think of is this:
his thoughtless young body,

kouros-tall and straight;
and the way he used to swing me

from the slender circle
of his muscled waist.

Paradise Lost

In memory of D. Cassidy,
adored 1971-73

Three years sighed out
in a luxury of longing.
Three years spent feeding
on holy relics:
a lock of your hair, news
of someone you had touched.
We trailed like pilgrims
to the Wembley Mecca, slept out
like Eastern ascetics
under the fig trees of porches.

Oh David, oh sacrificial lamb!
We touched the white hems
of your rhinestone trousers
when, once in a millennium,
you descended to earth.
Watched you pretend to walk
like any ordinary man, on dry land;
queued to see you work your spells,
making the calm woman hysterical.

You cast your voice like a net
and fished us up, in schools.
Shoals of us in the stalls,
heaped and thrashing,
our arms flung out like martyrs
waiting to be lifted from the world.
At home in our small rooms,
at private shrines,
a single candle burning
under the tired pouches of your eyes,
we chanted prayers, passed solemn hours

in the disciplines of devotion.
We feasted on the crumbs
of your transparent flesh;
nibbled at your eyelashes, toes,
your food-fads, face creams,
a sprinkling of spots. We put our lips
to the star-shaped birth mark.

Now you're a retired messiah,
sleeping on nails in some backstreet,
catching coins for tricks.
Your wardrobe's a mausoleum
of dreamy pouts and cowboy boots.
There's a fan letter once a week.
Sometimes you get mistaken for yourself.

The Big Things

The music of happiness:
from the kitchen, teapot and cups
clashing gently, in the first quiet
when only the birds, and we, are up.
And the look:
a coat, still wearing the cold,
flung over a chair back.

Rest

Your breast is the beach where I can lie
full length with my eyes shut
under the sun's warm hands.
It is the resilient tide
on which I can cut anchor and be carried off
like driftwood, swung and dipped
gently, slightly drunk,
light as a cork and blissful,
washed lazily this way and that
by the water's strong life.
Your breast is the sea and the shore beneath,
the tide's hammock and the tree
to which it is tied, slowly swaying.

The New Cat

First appears one March morning
when the wind is plucking the magnolia
fast, and the white tongues
are heaping like feathers.

She's slung so low
her belly's a submarine to the wall,
sliding after the periscope of her eyes.

If she could disappear she would:
would be nothing but an eye-needle
tracking a leaf's escape.
What she has discovered

is this continent beyond the house
where the air moves, and is criss-crossed
with a shuttle of notes
that pierce her with dissolving arrows.

One sticks her for a moment now
and she's sprung like a trap,
knowing not where or what
but anyway dashing at it.

Then the grass trembles
and she's lolloping
in sideways bounds across the turf,
spine electric, pipecleaner bend
of a tail squiggled up.

Now the ground's sewn with tacks,
and each step's a pirouette.
And that bush of malignant shape
must be stalked in mime
so it won't wake up.

But first there's a twig to ambush,
a spangle of light to poach,
walls to creep and overcome,
the torso of a cypress tall as the day
to grapple with, then scoot.

Morning Tea

My father was always the first down
soft, into the untouched hush.
The paper still silky on the mat;
kettle somnolently tuning up;
chink of glass on stone still ringing
in the just-minted milk.

Did he whistle then to himself?
That peculiar windy whistle
through whittled teeth
like the first quiet chuggings
of an engine settling
into its accustomed track.

He would be taking his time,
swirling the water like a gold-sifter
in the pot's broad bowl; judiciously
measuring the gunpowder heap;
stirring the brew, tapping the spoon,
deliberately fitting the lid.

Elegantly slippered and gowned
in my little box room he appeared,
only slightly shivering the cup.
He half-whistled as he set it down,
helping me off the night train,
himself not long alighted.